"With its variety of short poems o climate change and on Cornwall's book is an enjoyable read and will  is

Katrina Griffith, Kresen Kernow (Cornwall Centre), Redruth

"An intriguing insight into the landscape of a Cornishman's life - thoroughly recommended."

Kim Nicol, St.Ives Times and Echo

"A lovely collection of verse, by turns gently amusing and thought-provoking. Redolent with the atmosphere of Cornwall in all its different moods, wistful at times, but clearly not shying away from the challenges of the future. A delightful addition to our poetry shelves."

Bridget Bomford, librarian (retired)

"I loved the range of subjects covered by this book- you really feel like you've been treated to an all-embracing tour of Cornish life!" K. Prince, Cornwall Music Service teacher

1

By the same author:

Quizzy the Lamb – An amazing insight into animal behaviour (Amazon 2022

For more information, see www.poems99.com

99 Poems

A touch of Cornwall

By Claude Bennetts

This book is dedicated to the memory of my beloved son James (1965-2021)

Foreword

"Yth on ni oll war agan fordh hir
yn dann an howl ow hwilas styr"

"We're all on our long road under the sun - what does it mean?"

Claude Bennetts has indeed travelled a long road. He started on his journey during a world war and has lived through four generations. He began writing poems not that long ago after the loss of his wife and his son, to collect his thoughts and perhaps to make his own sense of the world.

Cornish men and women are often accused of having a parochial and a narrow attitude or outlook. Like so many generalisations this is wide of the mark and far from the truth. An interest in the place where you live and those that you live with, does not make you less interested in other people, places or situations.

This little book gives the lie to this assertion as far as Claude is concerned, for although his affection for Cornwall and the area around the Lizard is clear, so is his concern about our global environment. There is much in this collection directed at children and his observation of and understanding of animal behaviour comes through in his writing. The photographs in this book are both appropriate and excellent.

I hope this book encourages others to put pen to paper to write of their own experience and feelings, my congratulations to Claude.

Mick Paynter, Skogynn Pryv, PORTH IA
Former Grand Bard, Gorsedd Kernow

Acknowledgements

First of all I would like to thank my late wife **Joan Bennetts** for her encouragement when times were difficult and for all her recollections of our life on the farm.

Secondly I would like to thank my granddaughters **Holly and Sophie Bennetts** for their help in proofreading.

Also **Ann Sheppard** for meticulously checking the final proof.

Thanks are also due to **Rosalind Emo** for her contributions to this book.

I would also like to thank **Yarden Collins** for her help and support.

I appreciate the course run by **Raymond Arron** which helped me with the publication of this book.

Finally I would like to thank **Gavin Nicol** for all his practical help, without which this book would never have been published

Contents

Part 1 – People and places

What a beautiful day

The sun has risen from the East

Into a cloudless sky

The dawn choir now rings out

Across the countryside

Off to the beach I go

For some relaxation

To sit beside the calm blue sea

And rest upon the golden sands

Now that Summer has arrived

What a joy it is to be

In Cornwall at this time of year!

Spring

The winter storms are over

Spring is on its way

The trees are showing signs of bud

The birds are building nests

The daffodils are budding

The cherry trees in blossom

The sheep are lambing in the fields

The grass is waving in the breeze

The sunshine and the showers

Brings the spring to life

Now we can look forward

Leaving winter way behind us

Lonely

On a cold and windy night

I was all alone

All I really wanted

Was to get back to my home

When I arrived back there

I could not find the key

Then I met my pussy cat

And she meowed at me

"Where have you been?"

She said to me

"You have been away so long"

I said to her I will go and get your tea

When I can find that blessed key

I found the key and fed the cat

Who snuggled up to me

Now I am no longer lonely

Now my pussy cat's with me

Daffodils

I walked through a field of daffodils

Swaying in the breeze

Their golden yellow colour

Stood out among the fields

The raindrops on their leaves

Shone like diamonds in the sun

Young lambs were playing

While their mothers grazed the grass

The birds up in the trees

Were tweeting out their song

A frog was croaking in a nearby pond

I felt a sense of joy

That spring had just begun

Easter day

As I walked down pass the church

On Easter Sunday morning

The sun shone down upon the land

The sea was lapping on the shore

With its blue reflection

The birds were singing in the trees

A kind of peace across the land

Then suddenly the bells rang out

The joy of Easter just began

Then the village came to life

As the congregation gathered

To celebrate this glorious Easter day

Electric Light

I went to switch the light on

But it would not light up

I went to put the trip in

But it would not stay in

I knew I had a fault

That I could not fix

I rang up the electrician

Who said he could not come

Now I am left with candle light

Until I can get it fixed

It is like stepping back in time

Before the power came

April

On an April evening

As the sun was setting in the West

The air was still and calm

A red tinge forming on the clouds

As the day came to its close

The dew was settling on the ground

The birds had gone to roost

Darkness was slowly settling in

The moon came out to shine

The air was calm and still

As darkness loomed across the land

A quietness and peace that's very rare to find.

Thunderstorm

Dark clouds were building from the east

The wind began to blow

The leaves were blowing in the dust

Raindrops began to fall

Suddenly a lighting flash

And then a roll of thunder

The trees were bending in the wind

Between their falling leaves

The rain lashed down the floods began

The wind was storm force now

The cattle sheltered in the woods

The birds clung to their branches

Then as quick as it had come

It was gone again

The clouds dispersed the sky appeared

The sun came out to greets us

Learning to fly

I went to learn to fly a plane

Out on Bodmin moor

We then did all the flight checks

Before we went on tour

We taxied to the runway

And turned into the wind

I opened up the throttle

And we went into the air

We climbed up to 8000 feet

To practise stalling it

I closed down the throttle

And pulled back on the stick

As she went into a stall

The instructor said to me

Push the stick right forward

And open up the throttle

Then gently pull it back

Instead of stall recovery

We went into a spin

Things suddenly went white

Black spots streamed down my eyes

Then as we stopped spinning

We were diving to the ground

Then I pulled the stick back

And returned to level flight

I told my wife "I'm still alive!"

When I got home that night

Life

Our life on earth is all too short

Don't waste the time you have

Treat each day as a precious gift

Use your time in work and play

To help others have a better day

Your life is like a treasured jewel

Use it wisely while you're here

You only pass this way the once

You do not get a second chance

Do not put off until tomorrow

What you can get done today

Make a difference with your life

Leave this world a better place

For those you leave behind

Enemy Plane

I heard the sound of engines

Way down in Cadgwith cove

As the sound came closer

I recognised the plane

It was a German fighter

A Messerschmitt no less

Now closing very fast on me

I ran into a nearby shed

When terror struck my heart

I looked back through the door

As a swastika flashed by

Terrified I ran back home

Into the basement bunker

My heart now pounding in my chest

Sweat pouring down my brow

I sat there thankful

That I was still alive

D Day

On a June morning many years ago

We were going to Helston market

When the Army pulled us in

They got us out the car and interrogated us

After half an hour they let us carry on

All along the road military vehicles lined up

Soldiers standing by them their faces grim and drawn

Waiting for orders to board the landing craft

The faces of those men haunt me to this day

As many did not return from the landings

On D Day

During the Second World War, I remember our car being stopped at the Mullion turning by army officers. They searched the vehicle and checked our documents before they would let us continue to Helston.

Home Guard

Two soldiers walked across the beach

On their night patrol

Very little happened until the early hours

Then they spotted movement

Way out on the sea

Last time we passed this spot

There was nothing there to see

As they stopped and watched

A sudden fear struck in their hearts

There's something out there on the sea

As they lay down on the sand

Their rifles pointing at the spot

They watched and waited patiently

Until the daylight dawned

Then they could see quite clearly

That it was just a rock

This happened to two home guard soldiers James and Oswald,

while patrolling Gunwalloe's Church Cove beach

G 7

The leaders of the world

Came to Carbis bay

To try to change the world

And help to make it better

They did a lot of talking

Then they had a barbecue

They made a load of promises

We hope they will pursue

Vaccine for poor nations

To help improve relations

Reduction in pollution

To help with climate change

We have yet to see the value

With what they have agreed

The week they had at Carbis Bay

Will go down in history

The G7 leaders met at Carbis Bay, Cornwall in June 2021

Flora Day

On the eighth of May I went to Flora day

As I walked down through the town

I heard the band strike up

The dancers then appeared

From out of the town hall

Then off they went a dancing

All around the town

Top hats bouncing dresses flowing

In and out the shops

The streets they were so crowded

I could not see it all

Then the dancing finished

The fairground could be heard

I went and bought a pasty

And joined in the happy throng

An annual celebration of spring through the streets of Helston in Cornwall, on or around May 8th

Padstow Obby Oss

On the midnight hour on the eve of May

They sing the night song by the local pub

When the morning comes

The excitement then begins

As they sing the morning song

The old Oss leaves its stable

From the old Red Lion pub

Following the teaser all dressed up in white

Dancing and whirling its black cape all around

Followed by the drums and accordions

Beating out the sound

Meanwhile the blue Oss sets out the other way

They meet up in the afternoon

In the middle of the town

When they dance together

Round the maypole in the street

Then in the evening at the ending off the day

They go back to their stables – until the following May

Climate Change

Our climate it is changing in an alarming way

Small birds are disappearing from the rural scene

Large birds are increasing new species to be seen

Some plants are declining from the country side

Some are thriving more as the land warms up

New species are appearing on the Woodland floor

Butterflies declining some to be seen no more

The ice caps they are melting sea levels rising too

The air itself is changing less oxygen to breath

The tundra releasing methane like it never has before

Things are changing rapidly in this world of ours

Each and every one of us need to change our ways

Or we will face the consequence

On some future day

There have been noticeable changes on the farm over the last few years showing reductions in small birds, butterflies and changes in plant life.

The Taxi

I drove a taxi late at night

Down to Falmouth town

I picked up my passengers

And then the fog came down

When I got back to Helston

I could barely see

Then I dropped my passengers

Oh so very late

By this time I had had enough

My eyes were sore and red

It was now early in the morning

And I went off to bed

Tresco

I took a boat to Tresco from St Mary's harbour

To go and see the gardens

On this famous isle

As I walked through the gardens

The birds were singing in the trees

The flowers blooming by the paths

Some of which I could not name

The bees were collecting nectar

Buzzing In and out of the flowers

This tropical island is a real gem

As it sits out in the sea

Off the Cornish coast

As I boarded the Scillonian

To go back to Penzance

My visit out to Scilly

Will stay within my memory

The Rescue

The Helicopter hovers

Over the sinking ship

The crew were clinging to the rigging

As the winchman lowers down

The wire rope is swaying in the wind

As he grabs the first crewman

And winches him to safety

Up and down he goes

Until all the crew are rescued

Then as the ship disappears

Below the rolling waves

The helicopter returns

Back to its station at Culdrose

Trevithick Day

Camborne remembers its most famous son

Who built "The Puffing Devil"

Back in 1801

This first steam locomotive

Of the industrial revolution

This Cornish built machine

Has changed the way we live

A tribute to the Cornish men of old

Now Camborne celebrates

Its mining heritage

With "bal maidens" marching

Children dancing right around the town

To celebrate the Cornish man

Who opened up the nation

With steam trains on the rails

And cars upon our roads

Trevithick helped to make the world

What it is today

Torre Canyon

The Torre Canyon hit the rocks between

Land's End and Scilly

Its load of crude began to spill

Along the Cornish coast

As it reached the shoreline

The birds got filthy black

The seaweed and rocks

Smelt of the oily sludge

For three days it smelt so bad

We had to stay indoors

They caught the birds and cleaned

The oil from off their wings

Then they cleaned the beaches and the rocks

An awful dirty job that no one wants to do

An environmental tragedy

That will not go away

*Torre Canyon hit the rocks off Lands End on March 18 1967. This was
an environmental disaster, the worst Cornwall has ever experienced.*

When Things Go Wrong

What do you do when things go wrong

In this world of ours

Do you sit down and complain

Or do you try to put it right?

Sometimes there is little you can do

Other times you have a choice

Work hard to put it right

Or get depressed and in despair

If you get out and put it right

You will feel much better in yourself

China Clay

I look across the claypits

Near St Austell town

The pyramids rise up

Like moonscape from the ground

The pits they leave

Are mostly hidden from our sight

And then you come across a hole

Torn out of the Cornish ground

With domes of trees and plants

From all around the world

Something you do not expect to find

At the bottom of a Cornish mine

Most unusual to say the least

So they called it Eden

The area around St Austell is surrounded with china clay pits and high mounds of white clay from the open-cast mining

Lizard Lighthouse

I watched the lighthouse standing boldly on the point

With its light a flashing out across the waves

Warning all the sailors of the rocks beneath the sea

Then I watched the fog roll in towards the Cornish coast

The foghorn then struck up with its deep bass note

Warning all the sailors to keep off the rocks

Now they have changed its tone to a higher pitch

To stop the ships from foundering

Down beneath the cliffs

Mullion Cove

As I walked down to Mullion cove on a summer's evening

I could hear the sound of distant music ringing in my ears

As I got closer to the cove, I heard the brass band playing

And then I heard the choir singing across the valley floor

By now the sun was setting as I approached the harbour

When I reached the harbour, a crowd were gathered there

Singing with the band and choir near the fishing boats

I walked to where crab pots and buoys were parked

On which the crowd were sitting against the harbour wall

As I went and joined them there were two young ladies

Close to me sitting on a plank of wood, drinking lemonade

A portly gentlemen joined them by the harbour wall

He sat upon the plank the ladies were sitting on

They went up and he went down amidst a piercing scream

The lemonade spilt on the crowd, confusion all around

Everything went silent as people looked up and down

And the band struck up again as the ladies settled down

The Policeman

The policeman sat in a layby

On a busy Highway

As he watched the traffic

A speeding car approached

Off he went after him

Chased him mile on mile

Until he finally caught him up

On a long steep hill

Young man you are driving far too fast

The policeman said to him

"I am issuing you a speeding ticket

What's your excuse this time?"

"You will have to ask my father

For he's a man of means

It's really not my fault you see

I am afraid it's in the genes."

Supermarket

I went to a supermarket store on an August afternoon

I went to collect a bunch of grapes to put into my trolley

A black widow spider bit my hand as I lifted up the grapes

I gripped my hand in agony and began to tremble

Then they put me on a chair hoping I would recover

But I collapsed completely and fell down on the floor

As I lay there in pain, gasping for my breath

The strength within my body was slowly ebbing out

The ceiling started spinning round

And I could barely see

I thought goodbye world

This time you are going to die

Then I lost all consciousness right there on the floor

The next thing that I knew the ambulance arrived

They put me in the back, still trembling like a leaf

As I lay there on the bed in agony of pain

I realised my life would never be the same

A true story – court case pending at the time of publication

Strange Object

The stars were shining in the sky

The night was warm and still

A welcome peace across the land

As I looked into space

Suddenly a light appeared

Travelling fast across the sky

I watched it fall into the sea

Off the Lizard head

What it was I do not know

As I looked up at the stars

A meteorite, a satellite

Or maybe something else

It's still a mystery in my mind

As I leave the coast

COP 26

The leaders of the world

Gathered at Glasgow city

On a cold November's day

They came to stop the world

From warming up

They talked about emissions

They blamed the cars

They blamed the cows

They blamed the power stations

They talked and talked for two weeks long

And agreed to cut emissions

Then the arguments began

Who what where and how

Some things were agreed

But some things just were not

Which left the open question

Have they agreed enough

To prevent catastrophe?

The Oyster

Two men were walking on the beach

On a Sunny afternoon

One man saw an oyster lying in the mud

The other picked it up

An argument ensued

I picked it up, the oyster's mine

The first man calmly said

I saw it first the second man replied

Then another man appeared

A solicitor no less

They gave the oyster to Him

And asked him to decide

He broke the oyster open

And consumed it there and then

Then handed each the broken shell

You have eaten it they both exclaimed

To which the solicitor replied

That's my fee for the decision

I hope you're satisfied.

Monday Morning

I get up Monday morning

To face another week

I look out of my window

And it all looks very bleak

The rain is sheeting down

And the road begins to flood

When I reach the office
It all goes badly wrong

I open up the internet

Where more problems do appear

I know it's Monday morning

As there's very little cheer

Retired Horse

He had worked the fields for many years

Long hours in the days gone by

And then tractors came along

And they retired him

Out to a field of grass

Now he can relax

To his life of leisure

As he watches the tractors

Working in the fields

He is glad to rest his weary limbs

As he reflects on his hard life

Working In the past

Sailing

Sailing down the river

On a Sunday afternoon

The beauty of the Helford

Simply can't be found else where

The branches reach the water's edge

Kingfishers in the trees

Sail boats moving gently in the breeze

A time for relaxation

To enjoy what Cornwall offers

In these harsh times

In which we are forced to live

The Ferguson

The little grey tractor

That changed the farming world

As it replaced the horse

On most of Britain's farms

It became a common sight

Working on the land

Now things have changed forever

Down on British farms

Thanks to the little tractor

That Harry Ferguson designed

The Clock

The clock was fastened to the wall

Many years ago

It has been there when the sun has shone

It has been there when the rain has come

It has been there when winds blow in

Down the many years

It plays a different tune

On time on the hour

So you can tell the time

Without looking at its face

Now I have got old and fall asleep

It wakes me up quite often

So I have bought some ear plugs

Just to get some rest

The Seagull

The seagull sat on top the roof

Overlooking St Ives harbour

As he watched the visitors

Doing as they please

He became so very skilled

At spotting opportunities

For an easy meal

Then he saw a pasty

Being eaten on the quay

So he swooped down

And grabbed it with his beak

Back onto the roof he flew

With his ill-gotten gains

So don't eat by the harbour

As the gulls are watching you

The Fair

I went to Helston on a fine September day

To enjoy the fair

After we finished

Harvesting the hay

Down to the fair we went

With roundabouts and bumper cars

And entertaining stalls

Then we went back in the town

To watch the carnival

The streets were lined with people

When the carnival began

It came down through the town

Right behind the band

The children and adults were all in fancy dress

Then the decorated floats appeared

With many different themes

Followed by the cars and trucks

From many years ago

A very welcome break before the long winter settles in

The Internet

The pen is mightier than the sword

Or so they used to say

But now it is the internet

That really has its way

Its influence gets greater

With every passing day

As technology takes over

Social media is the way

With robot use increasing

As the years go by

The world has changed for ever

Let's hope it's getting better

Every single day

Fishing Trip

I was walking down to Cadgwith Cove

When I met three fishermen

On a sunny afternoon

Launching their crabbing boat

"How would you like to come with us?"

They kindly said to me

I could scarce believe my luck

"I'd love to go to sea!"

We launched the boat and off we went

Around the point near to Poltesco beach

Where we found the crabbing pots

Buoys sitting on the sea

They pulled the crab pots from the deep

And brought them aboard the boat

Removed the large crabs from the pots

And sent the small ones back to sea

Back to Cadgwith cove again

To bring the catch back home

I thanked them for the trip

And then I walked back home

To have a crab for tea

The Disappeared

Where are all the butterflies

Where have they disappeared

Where have all the small birds gone

Why are they not here?

Why are so many birds and plants

Not around today?

The plants and flies they fed on

Are no longer there

When I was young in the years gone by

They were everywhere

The American

He came to Cornwall for a holiday,

Drove around the lanes in his Cadillac

These roads are far too narrow for a car like mine

A few wrong turns later he became completely lost

He stopped and asked a Cornishman

How do I find Curry in these narrow roads

To which the Cornishman replied

"I have never heard of Cury

Sounds like you are looking for a meal

I don't know the way to Cury

I have never heard of it"

The American then said to him

"You don't know very much"

The Cornishman's riposte:

I might not know that much my bird

But I'm not the one that's lost!

Cury is a small village on the Lizard Peninsular

The County Show

Early in the morning in the month of June

I got up very early

To go to the County Show

As I approached the showground

I joined a traffic jam

Slowly but surely the cars moved towards the show

Eventually I parked up in a nearby field

I went through the entrance gate

Where I joined the crowds

As I walked around there was so much to see

I walked into the flower tent

The fragrance there hit me

The flowers they were beautiful

A fantastic sight to see

Time now for a pasty and a cup of tea

I sat down in the pasty tent

Glad to rest my weary legs

Now I felt refreshed to walk around the show

All around the stands I went

To see all things bright and new

Up and down the livestock sheds

To see what Cornwall had on view

Then I left the showground to join another queue

Time to reflect on my time at the County Show

The Dream

I dream of a world better than the one we have

Where conflict is no more, relegated to the past

Where armaments not needed and countries can agree

Where disease no longer plagues us as we live our lives

Where all peoples of the world can work in harmony

Where there is no pollution on the land or in the sea

Where the forests flourish and animals are free

Where animals and people work in harmony

I know it will never happen - it's just a dream to me

Tall Ships

On a sunny afternoon

I went to Falmouth town

To watch the tall ship's race away

I watched them move into the bay

Then the start gun fired

Then the men on board the ships

Began to climb the masts

I watched them in the rigging

As they unfurled the sails

As the sails unfurled

The sail ships came alive

Slowly they began to move

As the wind filled up the sails

Now that the race had started

The bay was full of ships

All were in full sail as they sailed away

A sight that's to be cherished

To this very day

A race from Falmouth, Cornwall in 1988

The Pilot

As I fly across the sky

And watch the land below

From Lizard Point to Michael's Mount

Then onto Penzance and Newlyn

Where the fishing boats

Are In their harbour sitting

As we leave the harbour

Land's End appears in sight

Next it's onto Sennen cove

With its lighthouse shining bright

St.Ives now comes into view

And then the sands of Hayle

On to the mines of Camborne

And Trevithick's land

Next across to Truro

With its Cathedral standing tall

Next it's down the Fal where Falmouth

Comes in sight

The sun's now setting in the west as I turn back home

I cross the Helford River

Then onto Goonhilly Downs

There is not another place on earth

Can match this Cornish Land

Night sky

I look up at the stars

Shining out the sky

Some are near and

Some are far away

I wonder at the galaxies

Beyond the Milky Way

The vastness of the universe

I cannot comprehend

I wonder if there is life out there?

On the distant planets

Surrounding distant stars

Space exploration has only just begun

Sometime in the future

More answers will be found

Until then I look in awe and wonder

Staring at the sky

In the early 1800s miner left for work early in the morning and returned late at night, from late November until February the only day of the week they saw daylight was Sundays.

My father used to tell me how at Geevor the shafts extended far out to sea – he said miners working those lodes could hear the sea dragging the pebbles around somewhere up above them!

Although there is still tin in Cornwall, the profitability of mining this and other metals declined and the mines closed. However, there is now some excitement at the prospect of mining lithium in Cornwall.

The Miner

The miner went off to work

On a cold dark winter's morning

Arriving at the pithead

To go down underground

Down the shaft he went

To start his working day

With a pick and shovel

To dig away the tin ore

From out of the solid rock

A pasty for his lunch break

Then digging rock again

Back up to the pithead

As the day came to its close

Back home in the darkness

As night time settled in

The same thing again tomorrow

Day on day on day.

Swallows

Now that the summer's ended

Swallows are gathering on the barn

Ready for migration

As they gather there each day

They will soon be on their way

To where the weather is better

Where the bitter winds don't blow

And the winter frosts don't bite

Then when the spring returns

They will fly back here again

Back to this Cornish land

The Ghost

I was walking down the footpath

Underneath the trees

The night was dark and cold and wet

With raindrops falling down

Then I became aware of footsteps way behind me

I stopped still and listened

But nothing could I hear

I walked a little faster

The footsteps now were near

I stopped and turned around

But nothing could I see

The footsteps now were close to me

As fear struck in my heart

When suddenly I felt hot breath

Breathing down my neck

I stopped and turned around

To see two horns two eyes staring straight at me

It was a big black bull

That scared the life from me!

Summer's gone

Now that summer's gone

And autumn is upon us

The wind is whistling through the trees

The leaves descend upon us

The rain is falling on the fields

The temperature is falling

The autumn colours cross the land

The swallows gone to a warmer land

The bees are back in their hives

Living on their summer honey

The insects have all disappeared

Now chilly mornings, colder nights

The sun shines low in the brooding sky

Summer just a memory

As I sit beside the fire longing for spring again

The Combine

The sun shines down upon the plain

Across the fields of golden grain

The combine moves across the land

Threshing out the ripened corn

The drone of its drum is heard for miles

As it thrashes out the grain

The sun is now high in the sky

Heat is shimmering out across the plain

The metal is too hot to touch

As the combine marches on

Man and machine suffering the heat

Now the grain leaves for the store

To see us through the winter storms

Threshing Day

The driver of the steam engine

Got up before the dawn

To light the engine's fire

And pressurise the steam

Then as the sun rose in the east

The team arrived to work

When everything was ready

The engine started up

Slowly but surely

The thresher picked up speed

When the drum began to hum

They cut and fed the sheaves

Into the spinning drum

Then grain began to flow

From the back of the machine

Hour after hour all the day along

The heat and dust was tiring

As the evening approached

It had been a long long day

For everyone involved

Autumn

The long days of summer are coming to an end

The longer nights of Autumn are with us yet again

The leaves are turning golden brown and falling to the ground

The combines move across the fields gathering in the grain

The swallows they are leaving back to their native land

The apple trees are laden with the summer crop

The squirrels they are busy collecting winter nuts

The fields turn bare again when the ploughing starts

Frosty nights approaching as the Autumn settles in

The cold and windy showers sweeping in again

I long for the summer days to come back again

Dark Clouds

As the dark clouds gathered

Across the winter sky

The north wind began to gather strength

Then the rain came beating down

The trees were waving in the wind

Their leaves got blown away

The animals moved into the woods

To escape the gathering storm

As the storm progressed

Things got even worse

Slates were flying from the roofs

Trees uprooted, crashing down

In the days that followed

We cleaned up all the mess

A day that is best forgotten -

Now we can get some rest

December Blues

The wind was blowing from the north

Bringing sleet and rain

Time to go home and get some warmth

A cup of coffee maybe tea

Maybe tomorrow the sun will shine

Bringing some season's cheer

As Christmas day gets ever near

With decorations fancy lights

Let's celebrate this time of year.

Frost

The temperature began to drop

And it was feeling cold

As the night time settled in

The night got even colder

By the time that morning came

The ice was firmly solid

Then the snow arrived

And settled on the ground

The skaters went out on the lake

The children built a snowman

I then went in beside the fire

Until the weather warms

Christmas

I remember Christmas many years ago

With Christmas trees lit up in lights

And tinsel glistening in the night

With carol singing around the tree

With the children opening presents

Their grandparents helping out

The family around the table

Pulling crackers by the score

Enjoying their roast turkey dinner

Followed by Christmas pud'

Log fire burning in the hearth

Heating up the room

The cats all fast asleep

On the mat before the fire

The dog had finished eating scraps

A time of joy and happiness

Remembered from long ago

The Winter Storm

On a cold and moonlight night

A winter's storm blew up

The wind began to circle around

The sea became confused

The waves began to hit the shore

The sea was foaming white

Water spouts erupted

In the pale moonlight

Five fishing boats went down that night

A dreadful tragedy

Remember when you sail your boat

Don't underestimate the sea

New Year

As the New Year enters

The old year's left behind

It's a time for celebration

A time to put the past behind

A time to begin again

A time to learn from past mistakes

A time to make things better

A time to stop and think

A time to improve relations

A time to help others

A time to help ourselves

A time for a resolution

A time to make a better world

A time to benefit us all

Welcome the New Year in

Ukraine

The war that Putin started

Was completely unprovoked

An attack upon the citizens of the Ukraine

Now the tyrant's war machine

Rolls out across the land

Firing rockets into buildings

Devasting towns and countryside

Killing men women and children

Who have done nothing wrong

Causing trauma and misery

Right across the land

Forcing citizens to fight

To try to save their land

Old men women children

Leaving their homes behind

Fleeing to an unknown life in a foreign land

A scorched earth policy at the tyrant's hands

In the years to come

The Ukraine will be rebuilt

The memories of the devastation

Will never be erased

Snowstorm

It was a cold and wintry day

When the snow came down to stay

A north east blizzard swept the land

The snow clogged up the roads

The animals and birds moved off the land

Seeking shelter in the woods

Now the blizzard is over

The land is gleaming white

Children come out to play

In the bright sunlight

Part 2 – On love and loss

Loneliness

I tread a lonely path

Now that you are gone

No one to share my sorrows

No one to share my joy

No one to share my failures

No one to share success

You were my inspiration

That made my life worthwhile

I no longer have the energy

To speed me on my way

Everything is an effort

As I go from day to day

Goodbye

The time has come for us to part

Your stay on earth is over

And now you're gone you can't come back

The door is shut for ever

I know you would have loved to stay

And spend more time with me

You gave your all throughout your life

Asked nothing in return

You were a shining star that brightened all our lives

A lady of integrity, a rarity to find

Our life on earth is all too short

Time passes in a flash

I thank you for the life we had and the love you gave me

Goodbye my darling Joan

My love is yours forever

Empty House

Now that you're gone I live alone

I miss your smile when I come home

To be with you when my day's work was done

I used to watch you by the lake

As the sun was setting

Feeding moorhens ducks and geese

The fish were jumping out the lake as they caught the flies

Their gills flashed brightly in the evening sun

The bats were flying up and down avoiding all the trees

A barn owl skims across the fields

The moorhens settle down

I used to join you by the lake as darkness settled in

Those days were good - they're memories now

I used to sit beside you and look up at the sky

Watch the moon rise up and stars come out to shine

Now your star is up there shining down on me

You're gone my love you're in God's hands

For all eternity and as I turn and leave the lake

In the evening gloom, I walk back home

Where my empty house awaits

Parting

No one is here for ever

We are well aware of that

But when the time to part arrives

It rips apart your heart

We cannot choose that time

That time is not ours to tell

There is no preparation

That's adequate to make

It's part of life we cannot change

We all just have to take

Sadness

The sadness in my heart borders on despair

I walk a lonely road like I never have before

I am wondering what the future holds

Now that you are no longer here

Time passes slowly as the days unfold

There is no one here to help me

Through this sad and lonely time

No one to share my heartbreak

No one to share my tears

The depth of sorrow that I feel rips my heart apart

I am so lost and lonely there is little comfort here

Maybe sometime soon things will change for me

Or God within his mercy will find a place for me

Grief

Now that you're gone I live alone

I miss you each and everyday

I miss your greeting at the door

I miss the smile you gave me

I miss your lips to kiss me

I miss your arms to hug me

I miss you through the day time

I miss you through the night

There is no comfort I can find

In this world right now

I have to get up every day

To face this world again

I can't describe the hurt I feel

Within this broken heart

Bad morning

I got up in the morning the sky was dark and grey

The first thing that I thought was what shall I do today

I went and fed the cat, I went and fed the dog

I took the dog out walking who didn't want to go

Then I met the postman with a lot of bills

The sky then opened up and the rain came down on me

I left home without my coat and I got soaking wet

The dog stepped in a puddle and he got muddy feet

Then I had to bath the dog and clean up all the mess

Then it dawned on me I should have stopped in bed

Part 3 - Children's poems

Fred the Cat

Freddy the cat he loved to play

With anything he could find

He found a paper bag and then he went inside

There he found a ball of wool which he pulled outside

This he dragged across the room to the other side

Rex the dog was sleeping there when Freddy woke him up

Rex grabbed the ball of wool and Fred got tangled up

Their mistress came into the room and found the sorry sight

And had to spend the morning freeing Freddy up

Buzz Buzz

Buzz Buzz was a honey bee who lived in a busy hive

She flew around the country side visiting the flowers

Where she collected pollen to take back to the hive

There she made the honey in the honeycomb

Where it's stored for winter for when the bad weather comes

Buzz Buzz lives on the honey until the spring arrives

When Buzz Buzz starts again, collecting honey for the hive

Learning to Ride

I went to learn to ride a horse

Upon a summer's day

I tried to make good friends with him

I gave him lots of hay.

I slowly got up on his back

But when they let him go

He jumped and bucked and stamped so much

My fear began to grow

I landed hard upon on the ground -

With a splash and hearty thud

I slowly got up on his back

All soaked in sticky mud.

At first he settled down a bit

Then shook his head and neighed

Before he threw me off again

He didn't like how much I weighed!

Pony

Ginnie was a pony with a mindset of her own

She broke into the garden

And then she devastated it

She trampled down the flowers

She trampled down the veg

By the time they caught her

The garden was a mess

They put her in her paddock

And they gave her a bale of hay

Then she went to bed

And slept the night away

When she woke next morning

She tried the same again

So they locked her in the stable

Where she is going to stay

Spoilt Rabbit

Chewy was a rabbit who lived in a Hong Kong flat

He did not have a lot of room - he slept mostly on a mat

His owner spoilt him rotten so he got very fat

One day when it was tea time, he jumped up on a chair

He stood up on his hind legs and saw a salad there

Chewy saw a lettuce leaf which he could not resist

When he started eating it his owner spotted him

He didn't tell him off - he videoed him instead

Then he put him up on facebook

For all the world to see

Now Chewy is the bunny star of the internet

The Bantam

Jeremy the bantam cock lived in the bottom of the yard

Every day at feeding time He would stand and crow

Then a large cockerel arrived to feed upon his corn

Jeremy was hopping mad so he flew at him

He hit the big bird in the face but it had no effect

The big bird flew back at Him and sent him flying back

Jeremy attacked again and caught hold of his wattles

The big bird ran into the nettles while Jeremy hung on

Later Jeremy emerged having won the fight

Then he got onto the barn roof and began to crow all night

118

The Barn Owl

The barn owl sat up in the barn

Looking out across the fields

The sun was setting in the west

And shadows fell across the land

He flew across the valley to the far-flung fields

Where he went a hunting

To find an evening meal

He crossed the fields from side to side

His plumage glistening white

Suddenly he swooped straight down

Where he caught his dinner

Darkness now was creeping in

The shadows now were longer

Mist was forming on the ground

The Barn stood out much bolder

Now he flew back to his home

Back to meet his mother

Quizzy the Lamb

Quizzy was a little lamb

Full of energy

She used to run

She used to dance

She was a joy to see

But if you ever turned your back

A problem she became

A constant source of trouble

That's why Quizzy was her name!

Molly the Cow

Molly the cow was eating grass

Early in the morning

The sun was rising in the east

The mist lifting across the valley

Polly collected Molly

To fetch her in for milking

But Dolly Molly's calf

Had not yet woken up

When they reached the homestead

Polly started milking Molly

When Dolly caught them up

Dolly charged at Polly

And pushed her out the way

Finished milking Molly

And then went out to play

Thomas the Cat

Thomas the cat went for a walk

Along a muddy track

He walked along the verge

Until he met a rat

"That's lunch for me" thought Thomas

As he looked way down the track

Carefully he tracked him

Until he got quite close

Then he pounced on him

And caught him by the throat

Then he tried to drag him

Way back along the track

The rat is too heavy Thomas thought

Then Thomas let him go

Thomas got back late that day

With very muddy paws

The Buzzard

I watched the buzzard from afar

Hovering over the distant field

Her eyes were gazing at the land

She looked a lonely sight

The suddenly she closed her wings

And dived down to the ground

Where she caught a lonely mouse

Moving in the grass

Then off she went back to her nest

Where two young chicks were waiting

Later she was back again

Hovering alone above the field

The Canadian Goose

The Canadian goose flew onto the lake

On a sunny Sunday morning

The noise she made woke up the ducks

When landing on the water

Then as she went a swimming

The ducks all flew away

The trout were feeding on the weed

And they went to the bottom

The moorhens disappeared

Into the willow bed

Then more geese arrived

And splashed down on the water

Disturbing what little peace we had

On our Sunday morning

The Cock Robin

Little Robin Red breast sat upon the fence

Watching the pussy cat staring up at him

Then he flew into the barn on a bale of hay

Where he ate the grass seeds for his evening meal

Then he spotted pussy watching him again

Then he flew up in the beams to keep a watch on him

Where he did a whoopsie right down on pussy's nose

But pussy got it in the eye and pussy was not pleased

Now pussy keeps away from the cheeky little bird

The Moorhen

The moorhen swam across the lake

On a cold and frosty morning

Her head was bobbing forth and back

Her tail flicked up and down

Off she went to join the ducks

As the corn arrived

Having had some grain to eat

She now felt so much better

She flicked her tail and bobbed her head

And went back off across the lake

Then disappeared beneath the trees

To sit back on her eggs

The Crow

The crow had built her nest in the chimney pot

When we lit the fire, the smoke would not go up

Then we found a chimney brush

And brushed the chimney out

The soot and twigs came down

The mess was all about

Just when we finished cleaning

The crow came back to roost

Unfortunately for her

There was a big black hole

Down she fell head over heels

Right down onto the floor

Then she stood up looking

For the front room door

Billy the Goat

Billy the goat was having a bad day

He ate the washing from off the line

He upset his owner who

Locked him away

He chewed the catch

Which unlocked the door

He now escaped and then he was free

Now he went wild

And head-butted the tank

Spilling its contents all over the yard

His owner came back

And was not very pleased

So he found Billy a brand new home

Out in the sticks, all on his own

The Tawny Owl

On a warm and moonlight night

In the month of May

A tawny owl sat in the tree

Right above my window

Then in the middle of the night he began to call

Twit to woo repeatedly

And that then woke me up

At three in the morning

I was not best pleased

So, I got out of bed and told him to go away

He then moved to another tree and started yet again

And he kept at it all night until the dawn came in

The Dove

I looked out through my window

As the sun set in the west

The clouds appeared an orange red

Glowing in the sky

The light shone through the trees

As the evening lingered on

Suddenly a dove appeared

His silhouette against the sky

Then as the light decreased

He began to coo

Joined by another dove quite late

A duet then ensued

I listened by my window

While their evening song rang out

Then suddenly they flew away

And quietness resumed

The Cockerel

Arnold the cockerel woke early at dawn

Just as the sun was rising

He stretched his legs

He stretched his wings

And then began to crow

He woke the cows

He woke the sheep

He woke the horses too

He strutted to the farmhouse

And woke the farmer who

Landed a bucket of water on him

Making him all soggy and wet

This stopped the noisy old bird

From crowing so early again

Two Little Rabbits

Two little rabbits playing in the sun

Early one June morning

They chased each other round and round

Until they both got giddy

Then they went to sun themselves

By the farmyard gate

But then a nasty fox appeared

Looking for his breakfast

As he got closer to them

They woke up and panicked

One went right

And one went left

Straight down the rabbit holes

No more playing in the sun

It's just a bit too dangerous

The Squirrel

As the days grew shorter and Autumn settled in

Bushy tail was collecting nuts for his winter store

Then he went and hid them on the woodland floor

As the days got shorter and the nights got colder

He built himself a nest to keep his body warm

Then he went to get some nuts from his winter store

But bushy tail forgotten where he stored his nuts

Now he was getting hungry and needed to be fed

So off he went in search of food up and down the trees

An then he found a feeder where the birds were being fed

There were peanuts in the feeder that he could not reach

So now he had a problem and began to rack his brains

Then he took a giant leap onto the feeder's top

The feeder swung from side to side but bushy tail hung on

As he tried to get the nuts he was hanging upside down

Then he started eating them and began to feel much better

Off he went back to his nest where he settled down.

The Cormorant

The cormorant flew out of the morning sun

Straight down to the lake

Where he stood, there on the bank

Watching the water just below

He stood for hours very still

Waiting for fish to appear

But the fish had seen him come

And disappeared among the weeds

But one small fish had not seen him there

And poked his nose out of the weeds

Snap! the cormorant caught him in his beak

Opened his wings and flew away

Piggy Grunts

Piggy Grunts escaped from his sty

And broke into the henhouse

Where Arnold the cockerel had a shock

And promptly flew out of the pen.

Grunts ate the food and broke the eggs.

While Arnold flew into a rage

To warn off the intruder

Grunts went off to the farmhouse

And found an open door

He went into the kitchen

Where he ate a loaf of bread

Johnny came back from school

And went into the house

Where Grunts was fast asleep

Grunts woke and charged at him

Right between his legs

Johnny was on Grunt's back

Riding backwards through the door

Grunts threw Johnny in the mud

Johnny was not happy

Chased him back into his sty

Where he slammed the door.

Good riddance! Johnny sighed

Mitsy and Popsy

Mitsy and Popsy were playing away

By the nice warm fire

Where they found a lump of coal

Which they pulled out of the fire

This then made an awful mess

On the kitchen floor

Then their mistress appeared

Who let out an awful scream

Mitsi was shocked and jumped away

Grabbing the table cloth

That came down on her

With a bowl of flour

Mitsi was underneath the cloth

Covered in white powder

As her mistress picked her up

Mitsi struggled to get free

Both kittens and their mistress were a sorry sight

As they now looked a ghostly white

Mitsi and Poppy were put in the barn

Where they will stay - to do no more harm!

The Hen

She woke up in the morning

She stretched her legs

She flapped her wings

And flew down off her perch

She went off to get her breakfast

With the other birds

Having eaten maize and corn

Her crop was bursting full

Next off she went to lay her egg

In the chicken coup

Then she went to dust herself

And walk around the field

Where she found some tasty worms

To finish off the day

Then as the light was fading

She went back home to roost

Where she jumped back safely

Back on top her perch

The Woodpecker

The woodpecker clung to the side of the pole

And began to peck at the wood

The woodchips blew around in the wind

As they fell down to the ground

The hole grew bigger as the day went on

As he hammered into the pole

The noise he made echoed around the land

As he went deeper into the wood

Many more woodchips fell to the ground

As he finished hammering away

Now he sits in the space that he made in the pole

With his head sticking out of the hole

Woody

Woody the woodpecker had a bad day

He was pecking a hole in the back of the house

He made so much noise he was driven away

When he came back they were waiting for him

They pointed their hose directly towards him

He was so busy hammering away

He did not see the water jet coming his way

The next thing he knew he was soaking wet

So he went off for his feathers to dry

Now he has come back to finish the job

This time he saw the incoming jet

He flew off to avoid getting soaked

This was a day he would rather forget

Two little kittens

Two little kittens were having fun

Playing with a ping pong ball

Until their mistress came along

With a vacuum cleaner

The vacuum cleaner grabbed the ball

The two little kittens sat there stunned

They could not work it out

Where their ball had gone

Their mistress cleaned the cleaner out

Found the ball and took it out

Dropped it back down on the floor

Now the two little kittens are playing again

With their treasured ping pong ball

Baby ducks

I rowed the boat out to the island

Where I found a Mallard duck

With six little ducklings on a nest of reeds

She looked at me

"Quack quack" she went

She seemed quite pleased to see me

As I went back to the boat

She and her ducklings followed me

In one long line behind the boat

When I tied the boat up

They came ashore with me

Then I gave them some corn to eat

Now they're back here all the time

Growing bigger every day

Quizzy's bedtime

Quizzy the lamb was grazing grass

As the sun was setting

Time to retire and go to sleep

As her day's work is done

The barn owl takes to the sky

And sweeps the fields for prey

Mist is forming on the lake

The ducks are gone to bed

Bats are flying up and down

Night time is settling in

Time to enjoy the peace it brings

Until the sweet dawn chorus rings

About the author

Claude Bennetts is a Cornish farmer who has worked with animals his entire life. At various stages he has also been a District councillor, property investor and taxi driver – all in his home area, the Lizard. Claude's writing brings with it a rare talent for observation and insight into the lives of the animals and of the places he has been surrounded by for all these years.

Prayer for Mankind

Dear Lord and Master of mankind

We pray you to forgive us

For the pollution we have created

And the damage done by us

To the world around us

For the forests we destroyed

And the habitats we have changed

For the fauna we have damaged

And the rivers we have polluted

For the fish we have destroyed

And the damage to the seas

For the polluted atmosphere

We are now all forced to breath

Forgive us for what we have done

To this world of yours

Help us to restore the damage

Caused by our human race

Tribute to Our Late Queen

The Queen was our monarch for over 70 years

The head of the Commonwealth of nations

A stabilizing influence within a changing world

Respected by the people of all nations

A symbol of authority throughout the passing years

Who gave us all encouragement at times of national need

Helping us to make the world a better place

Reaching out to all the peoples of mankind

Providing a focus within these changing times

A long life of dedication to our nation

A shining example for us all to follow.

Printed by Amazon Italia Logistica S.r.l.
Torrazza Piemonte (TO), Italy

42119368R00090